MESA VERDE

NATIONAL PARK

LIFE
EARTH
SKY

BY

SUSAN LAMB

SIERRA PRESS
MARIPOSA, CA

DEDICATION:

To the Firefighters who saved Mesa Verde, in gratitude and admiration for their courage, hard work, and determination.   —S.L.

MESA VERDE MUSEUM ASSOCIATION:

In cooperation with the National Park Service and Mesa Verde National Park, the Mesa Verde Museum Association assists with and supports various interpretive, educational, and research activities. Through an active publishing program and the acquisition of other interpretive items the association operates four retail bookstores in Mesa Verde providing park visitors with materials to enhance their visit to Mesa Verde and the Colorado Plateau. Proceeds from sales are donated to Mesa Verde National Park to fund programs the park would otherwise be unable to provide.

FRONT COVER:
Cliff Palace, winter solstice sunset.
PHOTO © TOM TILL
INSIDE FRONT COVER:
Courtyard at Spruce Tree House.
PHOTO © JEFF D. NICHOLAS
TITLE PAGE:
Square Tower, late afternoon. PHOTO © RUSS BISHOP
THIS PAGE (BOTTOM):
Wall detail, Long House.
PHOTO © J.C. LEACOCK
PAGE 4/5:
Square Tower. PHOTO © LARRY ULRICH
PAGE 6 /7:
Far View, winter sunrise. PHOTO © TOM TILL
PAGE 7 (BOTTOM):
Doorway at Far View. PHOTO © JEFF D. NICHOLAS

CONTENTS

THE PREHISTORIC SOUTHWEST:

Ladder at Balcony House.

PHOTO © JEAN CARTER/GNASS PHOTO IMAGES

My first visit to Balcony House was the last thing I did on a long day at Mesa Verde. I was saturated with information, footsore, and grubby from traipsing all over the mesa on a hot summer day. *How different will this be from Spruce Tree House?* I wondered, as my tour group followed the ranger down the trail to the pueblo. *And will I even care?*

We turned a bend and kept walking along the cliff under a sandstone overhang where it was cooler and a few ferns grew. Ahead and slightly above us we could see the long, sinuous retaining wall of a cliff dwelling curving along a bulge of peach-colored sandstone as smooth as skin. We climbed a stout ladder and stood waiting in a little plaza for the rest of the group to arrive. I looked around.

It was obvious that, although Balcony House was constructed of the same sandstone and mud mortar as Spruce Tree House, it is very different. It is smaller yet somehow more grand, fitted more tightly into its east-facing alcove and more difficult to access than the expansive Spruce Tree House.

The ranger showed us a shallow basin pecked into a flat stone just inside the doorway of an ancient room.

"On the longest day of the year," she said, "a shaft of sunlight travels down the edge of that basin at dawn."

I peeked in the doorway and saw tiny marks tapped into the rock. For an instant I forgot the rest of the group and became someone else, someone for whom great mysteries are revealed in a ray of light from the sun.

Then a voice broke through my reverie.

"Can you believe it? I left the sunscreen in the car!"

I sighed. The modern age seems too pervasive and too loud for the past to glimmer through it. Yet as the group began to walk again, a mother reached a hand out to her child as she would have done 800 years ago. A rufous-sided towhee sang from a nearby tree, as towhees have sung here for millennia. Time let me go again and I floated briefly outside of my usual frame of reference of driving and paperwork, phone calls, and shopping for groceries.

Mesa Verde is a wonderful place for this sort of time traveling.

Almost anything can prompt it: an unseen creature rustling in a fendlerbush, or an ancient ladle hand-painted in a black-and-white geometric pattern. Puffy clouds sailing across the face of the sun cause fleeting shadows, making our vision flicker and our perspective briefly shift. A toe-hold chiseled into the rock beckons our imaginations up sun-warmed stone.

Our ranger had her own suggestions:

"Smell the smoke from their cooking fires. Hear children shouting as they play. Listen to the sound of *manos* and *metates* as the women grind corn."

For most of us this would be difficult anywhere else but Mesa Verde, which is saturated with evidence of the ancestral Puebloans and their way of life. Everything here seems to be so completely interwoven, their homes integrated into the landscape and the objects they made reflecting the natural world in materials and design. Even one small observation can enmesh us in their world.

This sensation can be especially strong at Long House, which was perhaps a ceremonial center constructed in an effort to reverse a long drought. Pots found here were full of pollen, still used in modern Puebloan ceremonies. Long House would have been like an enormous *kiva*, or ceremonial chamber, and the foot drums in the plaza would have made the whole canyon reverberate. Standing here now we can almost hear a rhythm like a heartbeat.

The multistoried bastions of Mesa Verde seem timeless to us, but they were occupied for only three generations. Their inhabitants—like most people of the Four Corners—dispersed to new homelands toward the end of the 13th century. There is a persistent myth that no one knows where ancestral Puebloans went from Mesa Verde and other Classic Puebloan sites, but ceramics and other artifacts confirm the spoken tradition of the people themselves, who moved to where they live today: Ácoma, Zuni, the Rio Grande pueblos, and the Hopi mesas.

I like to visit a Hopi friend in springtime when we can go on flower quests together. Some mornings, as I kneel to peer at the tracks of a cottontail in the still-cool sand or examine the heart of a mariposa lily, I hear my friend's voice over my shoulder.

OPPOSITE: Beam and T-shaped doorway, Balcony House. PHOTO © TOM TILL

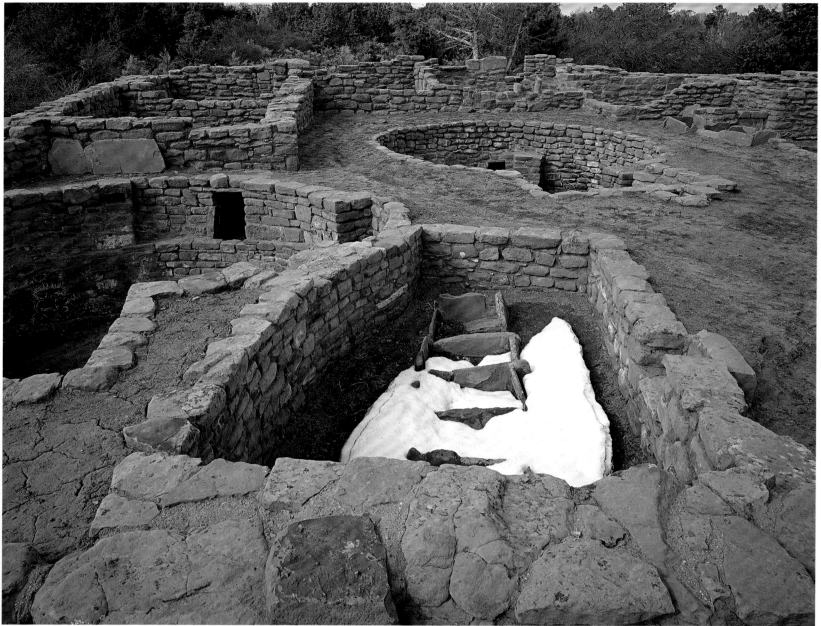

Coyote Village, Far View Sites Complex.

"Lots of rabbits this year; we'll have to keep an eye on the corn," or, "We always think of sunrise when we see those flowers."

I may glance up toward his distant cornfield or toward the east just as a horned lark perches on a nearby yucca. Suddenly, I feel connected with everything at once. Such moments restore my perspective and serve as a reminder that I and my kind are not and never have been the only ones to live in this part of the world. If only for a moment, I connect with other human beings—and with other creatures—across time. I like to think that centuries from today, someone walking on the same path that I am following will also hear a towhee sing and bask in a shaft of light from the same bright sun that shines on me now.

Manos, metates, and grinding holes.

The Wetherill brothers, from left to right: John, Clayton, Richard, Win, and Al.

The WETHERILLS

The story is often told of a snowy December afternoon in 1888, when a local rancher named Richard Wetherill and his brother-in-law, Charlie Mason, were out searching for stray cattle and caught their first sight of Cliff Palace. This event drew national attention to Mesa Verde, but these two men were not the first to find ancient pueblos in its alcoves.

The local Utes, of course, had always known of the old pueblos and had shown them to a few early explorers. In 1874, William Henry Jackson was a government surveyor working near Silverton. He heard about the cliff dwellings and made a private expedition to photograph them. As families began to settle in the Mancos Valley below Mesa Verde in the early 1880s, they also came across Puebloan pottery, projectile points, and dwellings. Soon many visitors, including New York journalist Virginia McClurg, came in search of ancestral Puebloan civilization.

The Wetherill story may be so famous because Cliff Palace is the largest and, to many, the most beautiful of the cliff dwellings. It was also this dramatic experience that led Richard Wetherill to begin collecting ancestral Puebloan artifacts in earnest. He sold several collec-

tions to museums, which publicized their origins, and visitors to the area hired him or another of the five Wetherill brothers as guides to the ancient sites. Before long, Richard devoted himself full-time to archaeology and kept careful notes and maps of his excavations, especially his work at Chaco Canyon in New Mexico. By applying stratigraphy—the principle that deeper layers of material were deposited before those above them—he discerned an earlier phase of Puebloan culture that he named Basketmaker for the beauty of its weavings. Navajos nicknamed him "Anasazi," their term for the ancestral Puebloan people.

In 1891, a young Swedish aristocrat named Gustav Nordenskiold arrived in southwest Colorado to see the Puebloan sites. He was touring the world in order to strengthen his health and obtain samples of minerals for his father. Running low on money, when he learned how much Richard Wetherill earned on sales of Puebloan artifacts he wrote his mother for help in financing his own dig at Mesa Verde. Nordenskiold recruited Richard's brother, John, to help him conduct and record a systematic excavation on the mesa, thereby introducing the locals to scientific methods. After Nordenskiold published his finds in 1893, he died of tuberculosis at the age of 24.

Both Nordenskiold and Richard Wetherill funded their work through the sale of artifacts. Although this would be considered unethical as well as illegal today, it was a common practice of the day.

CULTURES OF THE SOUTHWEST

Summer is the easiest time to imagine what it was like to live as a hunter-gatherer on the Colorado Plateau. The air is warm, flowers are in bloom, and we delight in glimpses of creatures scurrying across rocks or flitting from tree to tree. We recall the summer days of childhood, when to say farewell to the world outdoors and go inside was almost more than we could bear.

After a century of research, archaeologists and anthropologists now interpret the people of the distant past very differently than in the days when exhibits invariably showed a band of troglodytes huddled anxiously around a campfire. Experience with hunter-gatherers of recent times—particularly the Shoshone of the Great Basin of North America as well as people in Africa, South America, and Australia—has shown that being without permanent shelter or material possessions does not necessarily mean a life spent in hardship and misery.

In fact, one of the more surprising conclusions that scholars have reached is that foraging for food takes far less time and effort than farming (actually, this may come as no surprise to avid gardeners or present-day farmers). Finding shelter for the night or shade in the daytime is not nearly as much work as maintaining a home, especially a modern one. Social and family bonds are usually stronger when everyone unites in pursuit of shared goals, and more leisure time offers the opportunity to develop complex oral traditions and a rich interior life.

Although we find no evidence for people settling on Mesa Verde before about AD 550, signs of human presence on the Colorado Plateau date back at least 10,000 years to the Paleolithic (Old Stone) Age. The Pleistocene Ice Age had waned and the climate was becoming warmer and drier. Pleistocene creatures may still have roamed the region as late as 10,000 BC, possibly mammoths, giant ground sloths, shrub and musk oxen, and the once common Harrington mountain goat.

Early hunters used short spears with big, Clovis-style points that were designed to kill mammoths. Folsom points, smaller and more suited to the hunting of bison, came into use at a later phase. Neither type of point has yet been found in direct association with the remains of these animals on the Colorado Plateau itself, but finds from Palaeo camps elsewhere in the Southwest indicate that these big-game hunters lived in groups of less than 40 and killed their prey near springs and streams.

What is missing from this picture? Almost everything! Probably only a few people were fit and skilled enough to be hunters, and each kill resulted in enough meat to last for quite a while. Most of the time, people must have been doing something other than hunting. We have virtually no archaeological evidence to tell us how Palaeo-Indians passed their days, but anthropologists studying today's hunting cultures report that they explore their surroundings, tend their children, sing songs and tell stories, prepare food, groom and adorn themselves and one another, watch the night sky, and speculate on the forces of nature.

As the climate warmed and dried, plants and animals became smaller and less abundant. During the Archaic period which began about 8,000 years ago, people in the Southwest still hunted bison but depended more upon smaller game such as rabbits, sometimes throwing curved sticks instead of short spears. They collected leaves, roots, fruits, and seeds of plants in simple bags and baskets; sometimes drying or parching them with coals and grinding them between stones. People followed the migrations of animals and the ripening of plants from the lowlands in winter to the highlands in summer. As the seasons unfolded, every day was different. There was a need to know so much about the world, about the properties of plants and how to use them for medicines, dyes, and textiles.

Due to different conditions where they hunted and gathered, local variations emerged in the ways that people in different parts of the Southwest made snares, traps, and containers. No doubt there were other geographical distinctions between groups. On the Colorado Plateau, for example, Archaic people painted eerie, elongated, human-like figures with elaborate headdresses and garments on canyon walls. They bent twigs into the shapes of four-legged animals—deer, elk, bighorn sheep—which they then often pierced with a stick and left in caves.

Corn and squash arrived on the Plateau at least as early as 1500 BC. Corn had been domesticated long before in what is now Mexico, then spread gradually across the Southwest as farmers traded seeds and know-how with neighboring groups or moved into new territory themselves.

Archaic people of the region had long collected grass seeds and at first glance, corn is simply a grass with very large seeds. But corn cannot disperse those seeds and grow without the help of human beings. Nevertheless it took at least two thousand years between the time that corn and squash came to the Plateau and the time when farming became central to life here. Apparently, people planted just a few seeds at first, and either stayed nearby to look after them or returned in time for a small harvest. It wasn't until about 200 BC that some settled down in permanent dwellings dug into the earth, called pithouses. The footloose Archaic era was drawing to a close; the time of the Basketmakers was at hand.

The Basketmaker phase of the ancestral Puebloan culture was named for the exquisite baskets of all shapes and sizes that they made. They also crafted sandals, cradles, nets, and textiles of plant fibers, fur, and hair. People lived in rock shelters or in large rooms dug into the ground and domed with poles and clay. Instead of hurling spears at animals

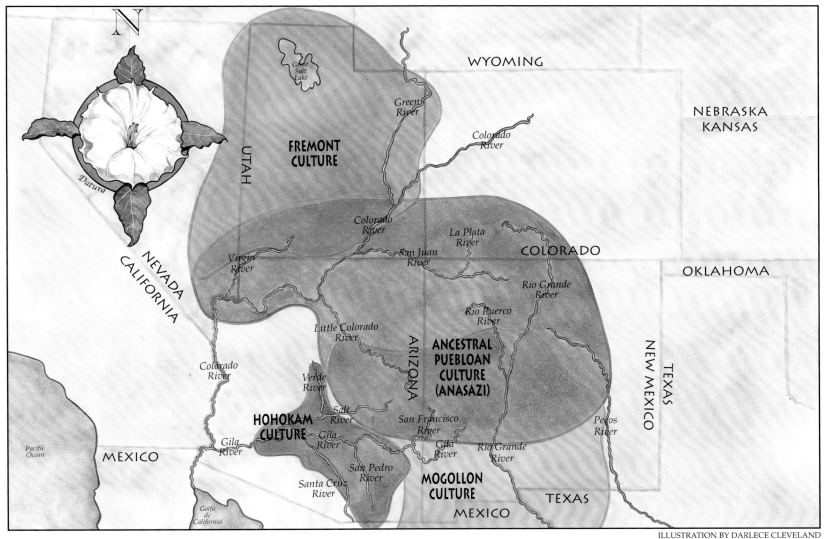

ILLUSTRATION BY DARLECE CLEVELAND

they launched them from carved spearthrowers, or *atlatls*, or flung throwing sticks at small prey such as rabbits. They obtained some pottery from the Mimbres people to the south through trade, but did not make their own ceramics until late in the Basketmaker era.

There must be many reasons why people began to forsake a wandering life. The population of the Southwest had been growing for years, meaning more competition in foraging for food. If they stayed in one place, people could keep an eye on the crops they had planted as well as on any surplus they had stored from past harvests. Having a permanent home meant having a place to create and keep tools, clothing, toys, and other artifacts instead of having to carry them everywhere. Dividing up tasks allowed individuals to develop particular skills, and a settled society could build complex structures and carry out elaborate ceremonies.

Farming also yields more calories per acre, although nutrition suffered from the monotony of a few crops instead of a range of wild foods. With the introduction of bows and arrows, which were lighter, more accurate, and more lethal than atlatls and darts, hunting probably required less roaming. And so, although the hunter-gatherer economy is widely considered to have been a highly egalitarian, stable, and successful way of life, permanent settlement offered significant advantages to a burgeoning population.

As people settled down, they adapted ever more closely to conditions in their particular areas and regional differences in culture became more pronounced. The people who settled on the Colorado Plateau are now known as the ancestral Puebloans (once called the Anasazi). South of the Plateau in what is now Arizona, there were other farmers referred to as Sinagua (Spanish for "without water"). In the hot Sonoran Desert farther south, members of the Hohokam culture built a network of canals to irrigate their crops. The Mogollon settled in the highlands of what is now New Mexico, while north of the ancestral Puebloans were a people we call the Fremont.

MESA VERDE:

Point Lookout, winter.

In the shady plaza of Spruce Tree House, the air is sweet and cool. I squint up toward the sun and through iridescent eyelashes, see strands of shiny silver undulating as they carry newly hatched spiders across the canyon. I try to imagine what it would feel like to be launched on a fickle summer breeze, to be caught up in an event far beyond my control yet occurring due to a wisdom that I am too tiny to appreciate.

Why does no one live in the beautiful alcove pueblos of Mesa Verde any more? Building them was obviously hard work, especially toward the end of the 13th century when ancestral Puebloans made extensive additions and modifications to many structures. Why did they labor over the massive complex we call Sun Temple but omit doors, windows, fireplaces, and roof, and leave it shortly afterwards?

We know that ancestral Puebloans flourished on Mesa Verde for more than seven centuries, becoming ever more creative in their strategies for survival. The more we learn about them, the more it seems that they had it all figured out—hunting and gathering, cultivating crops, dividing up tasks, collectively maintaining a water distribution system. Yet they left the mesa so abruptly that some people still think that they must have vanished from the face of the earth.

Their descendants simply say that there were signs that told them it was time to move on, that their destiny awaited them elsewhere. What sort of signs these may have been we non-Puebloans will probably never completely understand.

Archaeologists point to evidence for a 25 year drought leading to severe depletion of resources. Crops must have failed, springs of water slowed or stopped, and wild plants and animals become scarce. After centuries of gathering firewood there must have been none left for heating, cooking, or firing pottery. The numbers of people concentrated here during the Pueblo III period would surely have strained local resources until their economy completely collapsed.

Ancestral Puebloan society must have been severely strained as well. Only a few years ago, park archaeologist Larry Nordby noticed that a wall with no doorways had been built right through the middle of Cliff Palace. This wall may have divided the pueblo's inhabitants according to their responsibilities for increasingly complex ceremonies, offered in supplication for relief from rising hardships or perhaps as a means to bond the community together in a time of crisis. Or, the wall may have been built simply to keep the peace.

There is evidence of increasing conflict in the Mesa Verde region during the late 1200s. During the Classic Pueblo period, the population of Great Sage Plain may have numbered as many as 21,000 people. Most of them lived in cities, but there were individual families who led a hardscrabble existence on the fringes of society. Archaeologists refer to the former as *intensifiers*, the latter as *extensifiers*, and speculate that there may have been friction or even raids between the two when resources became scarce. Another plausible explanation for the evidence of strife is that non-Puebloan people drifting through the region raided the pueblos for food.

As part of a trade network that reached to the Pacific Ocean, the people of Mesa Verde were well aware of the wider world. When their life on the mesa became untenable they moved to the south and southeast, where water was more reliable and soil, wild plants, and game animals had not been depleted. Lots of Mesa Verde-style black-and-white pottery has been found in huge pueblos along the Rio Grande that were built in the early 1300s. The spoken tradition of modern Puebloan people links them to the ancestral Puebloans as well.

Were the people of Mesa Verde drawn elsewhere by more abundant natural resources? Or were they simply, as tradition says, obeying signs that we cannot discern indicating that they should carry on the migration begun when they—along with the rest of the human race—emerged into this world long ago?

Archaeologists place the Pueblo IV phase between AD 1300 and contact with the Spanish conquistadors in 1540. Today, 24 Native American nations regard Mesa Verde as the home of their ancestors. Each is heir to a different piece of the mystery. Just as people

Spruce Tree House.

of European descent regard history as an important teacher, each tribal group relates Puebloan history from its own perspective to teach specific lessons, such as that neglect of the natural and spiritual world go hand in hand and that traditions can lend strength to a community in difficult times.

When I am away from Mesa Verde, I think of stone pueblos nestled in cliff alcoves. But when I am there, I am most mindful of how points in the distance—Ute Mountain, Lizard Head, Ship Rock—anchor me in the otherwise infinite bowl of blue in which the earth is suspended. Clouds sail by on every side, shape-shifting as they grow until they are suddenly surrounding me, slapping me with rain. They leave the sky smeared with moisture, the rays of the westering sun gleaming silver in air and golden where they touch the land. From this lofty vantage point, I realize that Mesa Verde offers us perspective on our place in the landscape as well as on our moment in time.

North Rim escarpment and Montezuma Valley, dusk.

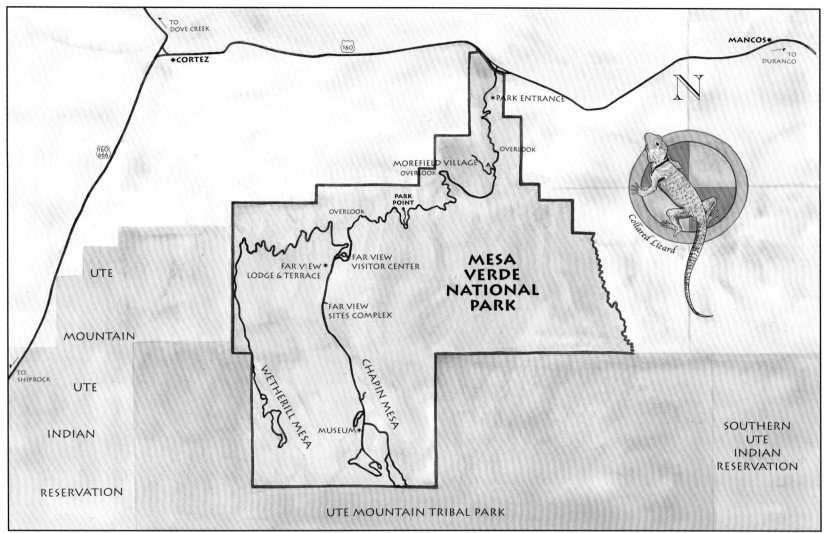

ILLUSTRATION BY DARLECE CLEVELAND

Local residents originally regarded the establishment of Mesa Verde National Park as an imposition on them by distant bureaucrats. Today, however, the park has a valued role in the local economy and has become a keystone in the preservation of regional cultures, both past and present.

After visiting Mesa Verde and other sites in the 1880s, New York journalist Virginia McClurg began to lobby for the protection of Colorado's ancient sites from those who would loot them for profit. Local families—who had been turning up artifacts in their fields for years—were offended by the implication that they were vandalizing their own backyards. But after Swedish aristocrat Gustav Nordenskiold sent boxcar loads of artifacts from Mesa Verde to Scandinavia in 1891, public demand for the protection of American cultural resources gained momentum.

By treaty, Mesa Verde belonged to the Utes, who used it as summer range for sheep, horses, and cattle. Although they did not tamper with the ancient pueblos themselves, they were unable to prevent others from defiling the sites. The federal government, as well as a group spearheaded by McClurg, made several attempts to acquire or lease the mesa. The Utes resisted until 1901, when Chief Ignacio and 11 other Ute leaders agreed to lease Mesa Verde to the government for 10 years. Despite this agreement, Theodore Roosevelt signed legislation creating Mesa Verde National Park on June 29, 1906, three weeks after passage of the Antiquities Act. This enabling legislation also placed all pueblos within five miles of the park's boundaries under the custody of the Secretary of the Interior. In 1911, the government obtained another 14,000 acres from the Utes, including Balcony House. The Ute Nation retained

a part of the mesa on which they established their own tribal park in the 1960s.

Over the past few decades Mesa Verde has become a cornerstone of the tourist economy, providing a substantial portion of jobs and income in the region. The park takes this responsibility seriously and endeavors to stay open despite storms, fires, and an aging infrastructure. In addition, staff of the national park and the adjoining Ute Mountain Tribal Park now work closely together, exchanging expertise and other resources in order to better interpret and preserve the ancient Puebloan sites of the entire mesa. In 1978, the United Nations chose Mesa Verde as one of the first seven World Cultural Heritage Sites.

FROM BASKETMAKER TO PUEBLOAN

Ancestral Puebloan people first settled atop Mesa Verde about AD 550, around the beginning of the era that archaeologists call Basketmaker III. Throughout the Colorado Plateau, a growing population was establishing new settlements, typically 8 or 10 pithouses with antechambers on their south sides. Compared to later structures, the two rooms of a Basketmaker pithouse were spacious. And although they would have been dark inside, they would have been comfortably insulated from the weather. Extended families lived in these little pithouse hamlets, probably the same families who had foraged together as hunter-gatherers. Hunting and gathering still provided most of what they needed, but they had learned to cultivate beans in addition to corn and squash. At Mesa Verde, they stored their surplus food in above ground rooms made of *jacal*, or mud-plastered sticks supported by thicker posts. They kept turkeys as well as dogs, made their own pottery, and carved bone and stone into ever more sophisticated tools, jewelry, and gaming pieces.

The hunter-gatherer way of life had relied upon a combination of providence and individual resourcefulness. Farming and the construction of buildings, on the other hand, were investments in work, the future, and the community. For some time, archeologists were unsure how the way of life on the Colorado Plateau had changed from mobile to sedentary. Had local people altered their behavior or had farmers from elsewhere come to the region? This uncertainty arose partly because peoples' very appearance changed during Developmental Pueblo or Pueblo I (AD 750–900). Their heads became flatter at the back; their faces broader. Eventually, it dawned on researchers that because settled women had more work than they had as gatherers, they began to secure their infants to hard cradleboards. This way, they could prop their babies in the shade instead of carrying them in slings while they worked. It

did them no harm, but fastening them to boards changed the shape of the infants' heads.

Most ancestral Puebloans of the Pueblo I period lived in above ground apartments rather than pithouses. The apartment complexes were actually villages with shared walls that were home to more than one family. Residents probably divided the tasks of daily life—farming, toolmaking, weaving, potterymaking, and so on—between themselves. Division of labor meant that each person could concentrate on their own work. Artisans took more time over the objects they made, painting elaborate designs on their pottery for example. With surpluses of food and well-crafted items to offer in exchange, trade flourished during Pueblo I, with cultures that lay far beyond Mesa Verde. Local people began to wear jewelry made of seashells traded from the Pacific Ocean and the Gulf of California. Weavers used imported cotton in addition to wild fibers, feathers, and strips of rabbit fur.

At the outset of Pueblo II (approximately AD 900–1100), farming conditions were marginal at best. The population of Mesa Verde declined for several possible reasons: families had fewer children, or they did not survive because of poor nutrition, or people simply sought a better life elsewhere.

Halfway through the period trade with far-off cultures slowed. Puebloan groups across the Colorado Plateau turned inward, focusing their efforts on building cooperative communities concentrated around Mesa Verde, Kayenta, the Virgin River, the Rio Grande, and Chaco Canyon. The people of these communities deliberately endeavored to meet their combined needs in an organized, collaborative manner. They shared resources as well as responsibilities, not the least of which were increasingly long and intricate ceremonies. Puebloan ceremonies of today—some of which are traced to Mesa Verde through spoken tradition—may be

described as collective prayers offered in exchange for the continued blessings of life and all that sustains it.

In mid-Pueblo II, about 1075, most Mesa Verde people began to aggregate into densely settled areas such as Far View, where there were dozens of large pueblos within a few hundred acres. They built near expanses of relatively deep soil on the gently sloping top of the mesa, at elevations where there were enough frost-free nights and sunny days for corn to ripen. Small shrines, and also field houses where they could briefly stay or store their tools, dotted the perimeters of these farms. By cultivating the soil and using many of the surrounding trees for building and firewood, they opened up the land and made it more appealing to jackrabbits, which they then hunted. In nearby canyons that were not suitable for farming, they continued to gather and hunt a great diversity of wild plants and animals for food and materials.

Although Pueblo II saw the rise of close communities with shared concerns and responsibilities, there were some Puebloans who still lived on the fringes of society in small homesteads. These people moved often, and the possessions they left behind were not as refined as things found in the towns. There is some speculation that those people who were not integrated into or dependent upon the towns created problems at times, perhaps contributing to the fortress-like character of later communities.

By contrast, town dwellers worked together to build great kivas, kivas that were much larger than those they had constructed in the past. Particularly at Mesa Verde and in the surrounding Montezuma Valley area, towers were built that rose above the trees and rooftops and were linked by underground tunnels to many of these kivas. Today, kivas are not only ceremonial chambers, they are also conference rooms where Puebloan villagers discuss the allocation of land and labor for other community projects

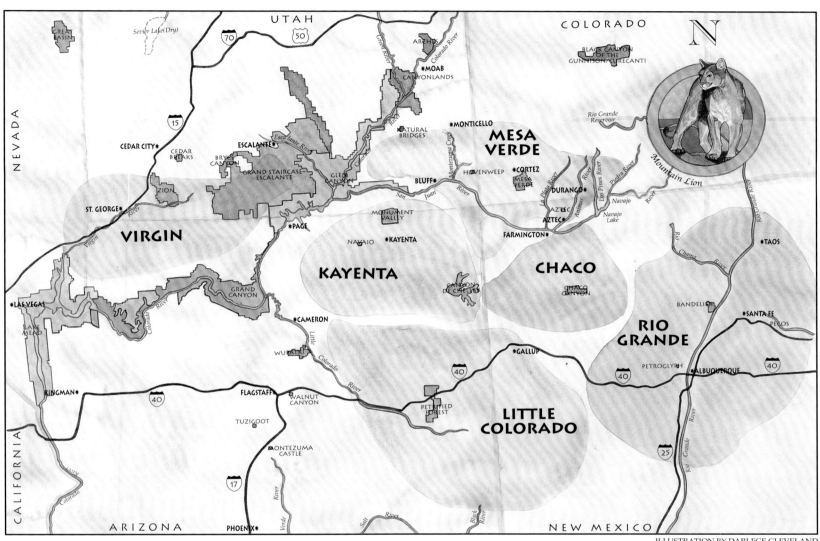

ILLUSTRATION BY DARLECE CLEVELAND

such as checkdams and farm terraces, reservoirs and water distribution channels. If the present use of kivas may be used as a guide, ancient kivas were a combination of church and city hall. Villagers met in them to make group decisions based upon spiritual as well as practical concerns.

During the second half of Pueblo II, very large Great House structures were built in and around Chaco Canyon, in what is now northwestern New Mexico. These were clearly the work of a highly organized group of people who devoted substantial time and effort to projects of monumental proportions: pueblos with hundred of rooms and dozens of enormous kivas, massive earthworks, extensive water distribution canals, reservoirs, and miles of roads. Oddly, though, they left

fairly shallow *middens* (refuse heaps) and few burials, leading archaeologists to suggest that the buildings were primarily for ceremonies, possibly done in an effort to reverse a worsening drought. In between ceremonial events, it may be that only caretakers lived at Chaco. By 1120, large-scale construction ceased there altogether. People no longer converged on Chaco Canyon, but there is some evidence of a Chacoan influence in the towns, roads, and great kivas that arose at this time on the Great Sage Plain and in canyons not far from Mesa Verde.

The people of Mesa Verde, however, seem to have been somewhat aloof from the outside world during the Classic or Pueblo III era (about 1100–1300). As many as 5,000 people may have lived on the mesa at this

time, but it looks as though they provided for themselves with local resources. Trade does not appear to have been a key part of the economy, and Chacoan elements are scant in the mesa's archeological record.

About AD 1200, major construction began in natural alcoves in the sandstone cliffs at the south end of Mesa Verde. Balcony House, Spruce Tree House, Long House, Cliff Palace—these were the masterworks of ancestral Puebloan stonemasons. Over the next several decades, each was enlarged, compartmentalized, and otherwise modified numerous times. Archaeologists interpret these modifications as evidence of experimentation with the way that Puebloan society was organized.

PAGE 20/21: Long House, Wetherill Mesa. PHOTO © TOM TILL

Trade items: Shells, turquoise, obsidian, and a *tchamahia* (probably used as a digging stick) displayed on cotton cloth.

TRADE ROUTES OF THE SOUTHWEST

Even in its heyday, Mesa Verde was a remote place perched on the outer rim of settled society. Yet the people who lived there wore pendants made of seashells from the Gulf of California, and carried the feathers of scarlet macaws from Mesoamerica in ceremonies. In addition to these material goods, ideas from far-flung places no doubt also found their way to Mesa Verde through trade.

And what did the people of Mesa Verde have to offer in exchange? In addition to, or perhaps *in* their distinctive pottery, they probably traded perishable goods that do not survive in the archaeological record, such as pinyon nuts, corn, and possibly hides or woven cloth.

Because pottery was widely exchanged in ancient times, both for itself and for its contents, its abundance reveals trading partnerships. The most typical 'intrusive' pottery found at Mesa Verde was Cíbola White, from Chaco and its outliers. San Juan Red, from what is now southeastern Utah, was also common. Although trading dropped off drastically by Pueblo III, active exchange continued with the Mimbres to the south and with Puebloans southwest of Kayenta.

Archeologists often know where a particular item came from, but it is difficult to determine just how it arrived at Mesa Verde. Puebloans still make pilgrimages to collect minerals and plants from distant mountains—pilgrimages that their tradition declares have taken place for centuries. They may have traveled long distances to other pueblos in the past, as well. A copper bell from what is now northern Mexico could have been exchanged from hand to hand, village to village, until it had traveled hundreds of miles to Mesa Verde. Trading expeditions may have set off with loads of various goods, trading with each town as they came to it.

Several elements of ancestral Puebloan culture are traced to southern origins: building techniques, ceramic designs, and most importantly, the cultivars for corn, squash, and beans. Among the Aztecs of Mesoamerica were *pochteca*, individuals who traveled extensively to trade. It may be that Kokopelli, the figure often depicted in ancestral Puebloan petroglyphs and pottery, and on a plethora of modern souvenirs, represents such a trader wearing a backpack and playing his flute to announce his arrival. Covering hundreds of miles at a typical walking pace of three to five miles an hour, without the wheel nor any beast of burden to help carry the load, such a character would have seemed heroic—even mythic—indeed.

OPPOSITE: Petroglyphs at Petroglyph Point, Chapin Mesa. PHOTO © FRED HIRSCHMANN

CHAPIN MESA:

Mule deer buck.

PHOTO © TOM BEAN

Mesa Verde's trails do more than link archaeological sites or offer vistas; they take us into the natural environment of the mesa. I like to find a place in the shade and sit quietly, imagining how the plants and animals might have appeared to the people of long ago.

Much has changed since the ancestral Puebloans lived here. Archaeologists tell us that there were very few trees here then because most of them were cut for fuel, tools, and buildings. No doubt it was quieter, too; today I hear aircraft buzz overhead and cars swooshing by on the road.

But some things never change. Chipmunks scurry about, sniffing and nibbling experimentally at every stick and juniper berry to check whether it is good to eat. A rufous-sided towhee scratches in the dust for seeds, a black-and-white admiral butterfly alights on a sneezeweed, a whiptail lizard pauses and then pounces on a crane fly. In a way they all remind me of human children, who also investigate constantly, often by putting things in their mouths. Perhaps any creature that depends upon the natural world does this instinctively.

I realize that it isn't the sound of motors that distances me from the ancestral Puebloans so much as my assumption that there is nothing essential for my survival here. My next meal will come from a restaurant, my clothes from a store. I know the names of the plants and animals and enjoy observing them, but my interest is a whim that I pursue only after I've been fed, clothed, and sheltered by other means.

By contrast, ancestral Puebloans found Mesa Verde an excellent place to live off the land. It was good for farming because of its relatively deep soils, adequate number of days without frost, and annual average of eighteen inches of precipitation. They did not subsist solely on cultivated food, and the mesa was also a good place for them to hunt and gather for variety in their diet and for materials from fur, bones, and feathers to fibers and stone.

Mule deer browse cool, moist slopes tangled with gnarled Gambel oak, ceanothus, fendlerbush, and mountain mahogany. Out on the warm flats dotted with pinyon pines and juniper trees, delicate pink fleabane, blue flax, and yarrow flourish among the grasses. Canyons sliced into the mesa are often several hundred feet deep, providing shade for serviceberries, sumac, wild rose, and currants bearing fruit that is sweet to squirrels, birds, and people alike. There is an especially rich mix of plants and animals where these habitats overlap.

Mesa Verde is high enough in elevation to receive adequate moisture for farming but also have a growing season of more than 150 days at about 7,000 feet above sea level. In winter, moisture-bearing clouds from the Pacific condense as they pass over the mesa, repeatedly dusting a few inches of snow that melt within a few days but add up to an annual total of ten feet. May and June are warm, windy, and stressful for plants and animals, but thunderstorms bring a welcome eight or ten inches of rain from the Gulf of Mexico during July and August. Storms not only benefit living things, but also replenish the water table. Rainfall and snowmelt percolate down to the impenetrable Mancos Shale, then emerge in seeps and springs that persist year-round.

Recently, I learned that a friend of mine, Eliuto Roybal, worked at Mesa Verde for the Civilian Conservation Corps in the 1930s. Amazed to discover this source of information in my own Flagstaff, Arizona, community, I asked for details of any restorations that the CCC might have done. Eliuto shook his head.

"My memory's not too good about that," he answered apologetically. "We did what they asked us to do and didn't think about it much. We were just glad to have the work. I liked it there, though."

"It's beautiful, isn't it?" I said.

He nodded, remembering.

"When you grow up poor, your parents are always telling you to appreciate what you can have for free. You know, 'stop and smell the flowers.' Mesa Verde was a good place for that. It always seemed colder where I was from, the San Luis Valley over in southern Colorado. People on that mesa would have had a good life."

I was impressed. Both Mesa Verde and Eliuto's boyhood valley lie at about the same elevation. Eliuto had worked outdoors

Oak Tree House.

in both places, however, and he could simply feel that Mesa Verde is warmer. This is because the mesa is tilted toward the equator about seven degrees. It receives more heat and light from the sun than if it were level. Plants develop earlier in the spring, bloom, and produce fruit sooner. Cold air pours off the edge of the mesa instead of pooling in low spots, making frost less likely to kill or damage tender plants.

Life a thousand years ago meant more than examining deer or rabbit tracks in the dust, it also meant listening for the snapping of a twig or the rustling of leaves, for the trills and cawing of birds. It meant catching the scent of a blossoming shrub, noting where it was in anticipation of the ripening of its berries. It meant feeling the warmth of sun on skin. It meant using every sense—sight, hearing, scent, touch, and taste—to make the most of this good place to live.

New Fire House.

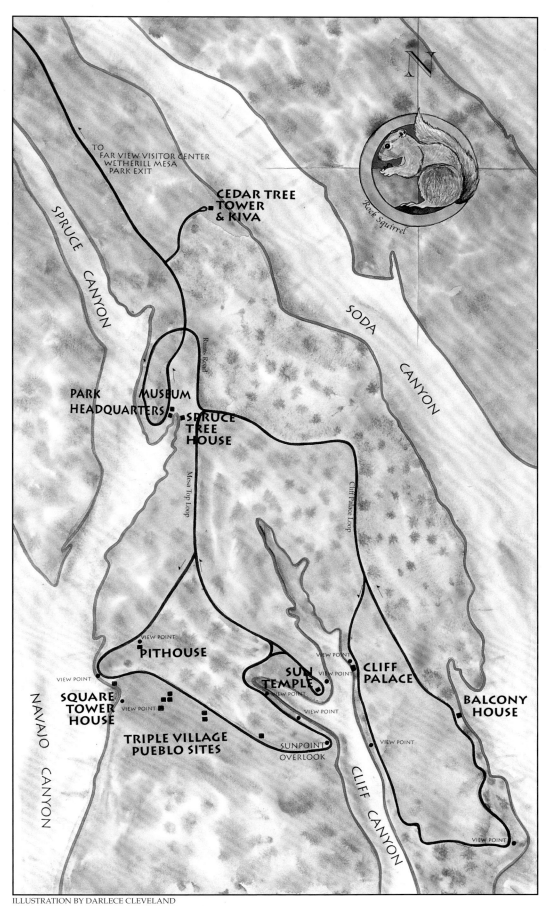

ILLUSTRATION BY DARLECE CLEVELAND

Mesa Verde National Park lies on a vast tableland, or *mesa*, that looms as much as 2,300 feet above the surrounding Great Sage Plain. Visitors approach the park from the north, where they stop at the entrance to pay their fee and obtain a map before driving the winding road up a steep escarpment to the North Rim. During the summer it is important to stop 15 miles inside the park at, Far View Visitor Center, to purchase tickets for ranger tours of the more popular cliff dwellings.

The broad tableland of Mesa Verde slopes down to the south from panoramic vistas. Park Point, at 8,571 feet above sea level, is the highest stop on the North Rim. Flowing water has eroded numerous long furrows into the mesa, isolating narrow peninsulas of land at its southern end. Just past Far View Visitor Center, the main road bends left to follow one of these peninsulas, which is known as Chapin Mesa. It was named by the Wetherill brothers for journalist Frederick Chapin, who publicized their archaeological work at Mesa Verde in the late 1800s.

Chapin Mesa is open year-round. The most famous and often-visited cliff dwellings in the park are here: Cliff Palace, Balcony House, and Spruce Tree House. Chapin Mesa is also where the park headquarters, archaeological museum, chief ranger's office, and several short trails— Petroglyph Point, Spruce Canyon, and Soda Canyon Overlook—are located. Visitor services here include a bookshop where the proceeds benefit the park, a gift shop, post office, public telephones, picnic tables, a cafeteria, restrooms, and parking. Wheelchairs are available for temporary use, free of charge, at Far View Visitor Center and also Chapin Mesa Museum.

Chapin Mesa offers a more in-depth experience than this brief list implies. All phases of ancestral Puebloan culture from Basketmaker III to Classic Pueblo are represented here. There are pithouses as well as cliff dwellings, farming terraces, tower kivas, modest villages, and even a panel of petroglyphs (images incised in the rock). En route to the more developed end of the mesa, it is possible to stop and explore the Far View farming community. This site—and the Cedar Tree area farming terraces about six miles farther down the main road—addresses many of the basic questions visitors have about how ancestral Puebloans farmed in this challenging environment.

Farming terraces near Cedar Tree Tower.

AGRICULTURE

It is sometimes said that corn created Puebloan culture, forever changing the way that the ancestral Puebloans lived. Once people settled down to plant and tend crops, they began to build permanent dwellings and places to store their harvest. Skills blossomed as they divided up chores, families accumulated more possessions, and settlements grew in size and sophistication.

The farmers of Mesa Verde usually planted near their dwellings but also at greater distances, where they apparently camped nearby to watch over their fields. Children, dogs, and turkeys helped shoo away rabbits, deer, and birds. Farmers trapped pockets of windblown soil, called loess, between stone checkdams that also retained moisture and warmth. In some places, they scooped out shallow ditches to channel summer rainfall to their little gardens, or dug deeper canals to supply stone-lined water reservoirs. They used a digging stick as a hoe to loosen and aerate the soil, as a dibble to make a hole and push in a seed, and as a lever to pry out weeds. To bridge the months between winter snows and summer rains, they planted corn deep enough to reach traces of moisture remaining from snowmelt.

Most of the harvest was dried so that it would last longer. To pre-pare corn, kernels were ground between stones into a fine meal. An unfortunate result of stone-grinding corn was the mixing of grit into the food, which wore down the teeth of the ancestral Puebloans and led to painful decay. On the positive side, ancient cooks knew that they must "lime" their cornmeal with the ashes of twiggy shrubs such as saltbrush to prevent pellagra, a vitamin deficiency.

They grew squash for its edible seeds and pulp and to use as containers, and later grew beans as well, which require warmer conditions than squash but restore nitrogen to soil depleted by growing corn. Edible wild plants such as beeweed and lambs quarters were welcome in these gardens, too, to be picked and boiled for greens. In traditional Puebloan agriculture, the line between wild and domestic is blurry at best. Puebloan farmers still welcome certain wild plants into their cultivated fields, which then take advantage of the moisture channeled there for the benefit of the corn. Domestication is a two-way street: we not only adopt other living things for our own needs, we are also adopted by them to serve theirs. This sense of a mutualism between plants, animals, and people remains at the heart of the Puebloan view of life to this day.

OPPOSITE: Mummy Lake, Far View Site Complex. PHOTO © JEFF NICHOLAS

THE WALLS OF FAR VIEW.   PHOTO © JEFF D. NICHOLAS

CEDAR TREE TOWER.   PHOTO © TOM BEAN

SPRUCE TREE HOUSE.   PHOTO © STEVE MOHLENCAMP

SQUARE TOWER.   PHOTO © RUSS BISHOP

Most visitors to Chapin Mesa stop at every opportunity to soak up whatever insights that particular location offers. Those who have less time or prefer to focus on certain interests may want to plan their visit around specific sites and ranger-led activities. Cliff Palace, the most famous of the cliff dwellings, and Balcony House both require a ticket for admission.

FAR VIEW SITE COMPLEX

This half-mile drive leads from the Chapin Mesa Road to this community of the Pueblo II and III eras (approximately 900-1300), an excellent place to appreciate ancient Puebloan farming and irrigation techniques. Early archeologist and park superintendent Jesse Walter Fewkes named the largest pueblo "Far View" for its sweeping vistas.

Here at 7,700 feet above sea level, the frost-free season balanced with enough rain and snow to permit farming. Far View House, with two stories and several kivas, may have been an administrative center. Pipe Shrine House and Coyote Village were built and modified from 900 to 1300. Each had 30 to 40 rooms in two stories, and kivas with towers and perhaps tunnels. Megalithic House and Far View Tower, built in the 1200s, are smaller. The most unusual feature here is a 90-foot circular basin built in Pueblo II and later modified. It may have stored water channeled to it by ditches. An alternative hypothesis suggests Mummy Lake was an amphitheater for the performance of ceremonies.

CEDAR TREE TOWER

A half-mile down this road is a one-mile loop trail through a shady oak and pine forest, leading to terraces built across a natural drainage to capture water and soil for farming. Farther down the road, Cedar Tree Tower could have been a platform to view the horizon as well as the starry night sky. Modern Puebloans time some night ceremonies by the movement of constellations across openings in their kiva roofs. This combination of ancient tower and kiva suggests that they did the same in ancient times.

SPRUCE TREE HOUSE

Visitors may explore Spruce Tree House and its setting at their leisure, without a ranger. Here they can appreciate many aspects of ancestral Puebloan life more vividly, perhaps, than at any other site within the park. The pueblo itself is Mesa Verde's best-preserved cliff dwelling with more than 100 rooms and eight kivas, one of which visitors may enter by means of a ladder. A year-round spring lies just a few yards away and the enclosing canyon supports a lively assortment of plants and animals that the pueblos's inhabitants once gathered and hunted. Nearby, a 2.3-mile loop trail leads to Petroglyph Point, where a panel of ancient images pecked into the solid rock of the canyon wall offers a glimpse of the interior lives of ancestral Puebloan people.

SQUARE TOWER HOUSE

Although Square Tower House is not accessible to today's visitors, the road-side view of this cliff dwelling is one of the most picturesque sights in the park. The pueblo is tucked into one of many alcoves eroded into the cliffs of Mesa Verde. A combination of geological processes creates these alcoves. Rainwater and melted snow seep through the pourous sandstone, dissolving the calcium carbonate that cements its grains of sand together. In winter this water freezes, prying off more flakes of stone to create large open pockets in the cliffs.

PITHOUSES AND EARLY PUEBLOAN VILLAGES

Early and late pithouses and pueblos along the Mesa Top Drive illustrate the evolution of Puebloan architecture—the first site is also the earliest: a typical pithouse built around 550-600. Pithouses evolved in two directions: into kivas, ceremonial rooms dug into the ground; and into pueblos, or dwellings built above ground. At one site here, a pueblo was built on top of a previous one every hundred years or so, showing increasing refinement in workmanship and complexity in social organization.

SUN TEMPLE

This roofless but thickwalled structure has been the focus of much speculation. It may have been a ceremonial center, perhaps related to astronomical observations made from Cliff Palace. It was built late in Pueblo III, when this part of the mesa was very densely populated.

CLIFF PALACE

With 150 rooms, Cliff Palace is the largest cliff dwelling in North America. In the late 1990s, its every detail was recorded in a database in the first study of the pueblo in 80 years. Its residents made many changes in the pueblo over the few decades it was occupied, suggesting shifts in the organization of their society as they struggled to cope with drought.

BALCONY HOUSE

Most cliff dwellings face south to take advantage of the sun's warmth in winter, but Balcony House faces east, toward the sunrise. There are a number of shallow basins pecked into the floors of its rooms, which are thought to be associated with the observation of astronomical events. Built late in Pueblo III like Cliff Palace, Balcony House was also divided in half by a wall. Its name comes from a narrow ledge built along the face of a room in its northern half. Balcony House may have housed about 50 people, or it may have served chiefly as a ceremonial center.

PITHOUSE ATOP CHAPIN MESA. PHOTO © CAROL POLICH

SUN TEMPLE. PHOTO © GEORGE WUERTHNER

CLIFF PALACE. PHOTO © LAURENCE PARENT

BALCONY HOUSE. PHOTO © DICK DIETRICH

Supt. Chester Thomas, Douglas Osborne, and Jean Pinkley examine pottery from the Wetherill Mesa Project.

PHOTO COURTESY OF NPS, MESA VERDE COLLECTION

POTTERY

Pottery can make the past come alive. When we spot a potsherd on the ground, it can seem like finding the footprint of a Puebloan person in the dust. Occasionally, we see the delicate impressions of fingertips on the surface of a piece.

Archaeologists re-create the life of an ancient pot using a combination of clues, from its shape and decoration to chemical and mineral analysis that determine the sources of its clay and paint. And because tradition has always been a strong force in Puebloan ceramics, they also seek information from modern Pueblo potters.

As early as AD 470, people around Mesa Verde used Rosa Brown, a rust-colored ware traded from Mimbres people of New Mexico. Puebloans tried molding clay into similar shapes but their pieces turned gray instead of red during the firing process. A few tried coating their pots with powdered ochre but this "fugitive red" rubbed off easily.

Mesa Verde artisans experimented with materials and techniques, creating ceramics that reflected their own culture's sense of what was useful and pretty. They dug fine clay from local shale deposits, then kneaded in a temper of pulverized volcanic rock, crushed potsherds, or sand to keep their pots from cracking in the fire. Next, they built a vessel of the desired size and shape by coiling up thin snakes of clay, then scraped it smooth with a gourd rind. After it dried, they polished their pot using a very smooth stone. Suitable stones were difficult to find on Mesa Verde, but stones worn smooth in the gizzards of dinosaurs could be obtained from McElmo Canyon to the west.

By 750, Mesa Verde potters dabbed white slip on gray-white pots to create a background to decorate with yucca fiber brushes dipped in paint made of powdered minerals or boiled plant juice that turned black in the fire. They had become masters of the firing process. During Pueblo II, they made both gray and red pottery and began to dent the coils of some jars in a style known as Mancos Corrugated.

Pueblo III potters combined mineral and plant-based paints with sophisticated firing technique to create *polychrome*—multicolored—pots as well as black-on-white ware. Mugs and kiva jars, two shapes that are unique to Mesa Verde, may have had strictly ceremonial use. The beautifully balanced geometric designs on Pueblo III pottery resembled the finely patterned baskets for which their ancestors were named.

OPPOSITE: Re-constructed Puebloan pottery. PHOTO © TOM BEAN

WETHERILL MESA:

Re-constructed pithouse, Step House.

Not long ago, I invited my friends Bob and Ruth to meet me at Mesa Verde for a few days. I thought they would be interested in learning about the people who farmed there eight centuries ago. Bob and Ruth, who are from Iowa, once farmed corn and beans themselves. But Bob looked doubtful.

"Why would we want to go *there*?" he asked, laughing.

Before I could think of an answer, he remembered suddenly:

"Oh! There'll be a full moon tonight; we should watch for it."

I thought of Mesa Verde again, and how the people who once lived there also watched the sky. We refer to them as ancestral Puebloans because their descendants are the Pueblo people of New Mexico and Arizona, who observe many traditions that date back countless generations. I remarked that calendars developed in ancestral Puebloan times can predict complicated celestial events that happen only once in a human generation.

Bob sat back in his chair and stared into space. "It never occurred to me," he said at last, "that subsistence farmers ever thought about anything besides how to get their next mouthful."

His comment illustrates one of the fundamental tensions in archaeology, which is how much our assumptions can influence our interpretation of the past. In our day, family farmers can barely hang on. We gaze astounded at the cliff dwellings, unable to imagine surviving in such a place, let alone being concerned with anything so sophisticated as astronomy.

"How did they do it?" we ask over and over, and the park service interpreters patiently explain again about the wild foods, the farming of corn and squash and beans, the springs and alcove seeps that provided water. Still, we feel as though a key part of the explanation must be missing. What kept people going? Wouldn't the difficulties have been overwhelming? Did anybody ever have any fun? It is as though we have lost faith in the possibility that the land we live on could provide everything we need.

Archaeology is a science based upon the examination of physical material, and researchers can extract an amazing amount of information from a wide array of finds. They can microscopically examine pollen and bones preserved in ancient dwellings to learn which wild and domesticated plants and animals were available for food. From the design, paint, clay, and temper of a piece of pottery, they know when and where it was made and by whom; they can identify the mountain where a chip of obsidian used to make a spear point originated. They find discarded artifacts from sandals to tools in middens, the refuse heaps heaped not far from dwellings. It is now routine to core-sample ancient roofbeams in order to expose patterns of thick and thin tree rings, then compare them to a chart of such patterns to establish the exact year the beams were cut.

But archaeology is more subject to interpretation than other sciences are. Only so much data can be accumulated before tricky questions emerge. Did the people of the past do things the way that we would do them in the same situation? Did each family harvest their own food or was the labor divided so that just a few people spent time gathering berries or tending cornfields? Why was a certain type of wood used in a structure? Was the wood simply handy or was there another, perhaps symbolic, reason? Do we find pottery and stone from distant places at Mesa Verde because someone deliberately set off to carry it all the way to Cliff Palace or only because it happened to end up there after being traded randomly from village to village?

Interpretation of the facts can range from wild to conservative. Southwestern archaeology is a continuously boiling stew of new information, personal theories, revelations from modern Pueblo people, sensationalism, common sense, and instinct. Evidence is interpreted and reinterpreted by careful scholars, wishful thinkers, and fierce cynics. Hypotheses are proposed, argued, and discarded. And yet, the overall picture does become clearer, year by year.

I first began to study ancestral Puebloan culture seriously in the early 1980s, when I was a park ranger. I was working at the Grand Canyon, where Puebloans had lived during the same time they lived on Mesa Verde. My previous park service assignment had been in a large city and I assumed that

Walls at Long House.

before the stresses of modern life, these people must have lived in a sort of American Eden free of pointless anxiety and conflict. In those days, many archaeologists held a similarly rosy view of ancestral Puebloan society.

Today we have more archaeological material to evaluate and better ways of comparing ancient and modern societies. Our interpretation of the Puebloan past now incorporates evidence of conflict and the exhaustion of natural resources. We take Puebloan morality tales more seriously and realize that the consequences they describe are based upon actual experiences.

One of the intriguing things about archaeology is what it tells us about our own outlook on the world. Our understanding of how ancestral Puebloans lived at Mesa Verde can never be complete. But as we endeavor to learn what we can about them, we have the opportunity to balance what we would like to believe—about our own way of life as well as about theirs—with the evidence.

Mug House.

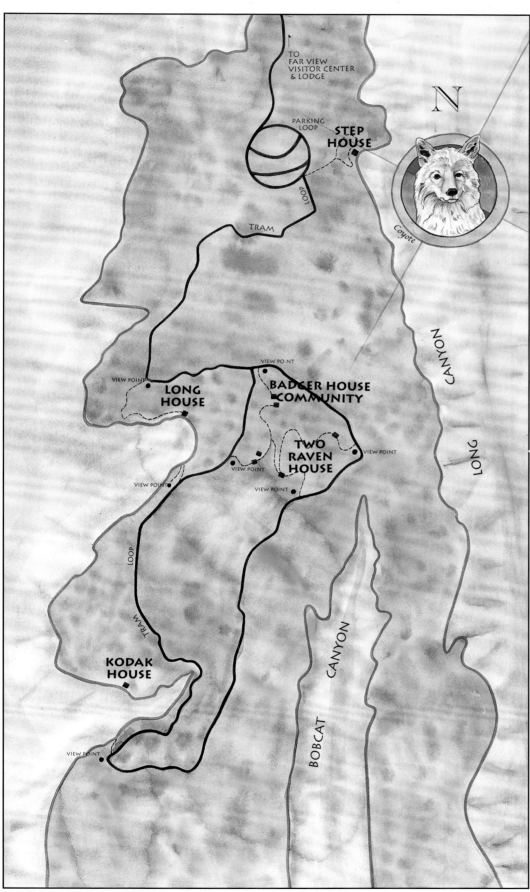

ILLUSTRATION BY DARLECE CLEVELAND

Wetherill Mesa is open from 9:00 a.m. to 4:30 p.m. during the summer season only. It is reached by a winding, 12 mile road that twists up and down over the landscape; only vehicles less than 25 feet in length are permitted. The turn for Wetherill Mesa is located on the main road just past Far View Visitor Center, where visitors may buy tickets to visit Long House, the second-largest cliff dwelling in the park. Long House is accessible only on a scheduled tour in the company of a ranger and tickets are not available at the site.

Wetherill Mesa was severely burned in the Pony Fire of 2000. Where the land was cloaked in oak scrub, regeneration of the vegetation had begun within weeks of the fire, but the pinyon-juniper woodland may take fifty years or more to recover fully. The fire swept over the top of the mesa, destroying all visitor amenities and damaging the modern structures that protect Badger House, as well as scorching the upper rim of the alcove in which Step House lies. Repairs and improvements will take years, but eventually there will be a ranger office, bookshop, restrooms, and refreshment stand in accord with the park's Master Plan. The park newspaper, *Mesa Verde National Park Visitor Guide*, has current information on sites and activities on Wetherill Mesa.

The relatively deep soil and the weather at this elevation of around 7,200 feet were good for farming in ancestral Puebloan times. In one quarter-mile area, there are more than 100 farming terraces. A 1958 survey counted nearly 900 dwelling sites on Wetherill Mesa, and many more have come to light since the fires of the summer of 2000 burned vast swathes of the pinyon-juniper forest.

From the parking lot at the end of the Wetherill Mesa Road, visitors may follow foot trails to visit several sites, or just take the free tram, or combine the two. The tram stops at pithouse and pueblo villages on top of the mesa first, then at the head of the trail to Long House for those visitors who have obtained tickets to the ranger-led tour, and finally at two points where there are views of cliff dwellings.

EXCAVATED PITHOUSE, STEP HOUSE.   PHOTO © TOM BEAN

LONG HOUSE.   PHOTO © J.C. LEACOCK

KIVA, BADGER HOUSE COMMUNITY.   PHOTO © JIM WILSON

KODAK HOUSE.   PHOTO © JEFF D. NICHOLAS

The top of Wetherill Mesa presents a stark vista since the Pony Fire of 2000 incinerated the pinyon-juniper forest here. However, it is still possible to visit the mesa-top sites around the Badger House Community on foot and to take the tram to Long House. Unfortunately, the rock alcove around Step House was scorched by the fire, and sandstone flakes off onto the only possible path to the site. IF AND WHEN THIS CONDITION CAN BE STABILIZED, VISITORS WILL AGAIN BE ALLOWED TO APPROACH STEP HOUSE.

STEP HOUSE

Some of Mesa Verde's natural rock alcoves were occupied from the beginning of settlement here. Although most people of the Basketmaker era lived on the mesa top, there are Basketmaker III pithouses in Step House Alcove, which made up a village of perhaps 25 people. A few yards away, there is a Classic Pueblo cliff dwelling for about 30 or 40 people, which dates to around 1226. The tunnel between its kiva and an above-ground room was blocked up during the time that the Puebloans lived here. One of the largest concentrations of petroglyphs found in the park was tapped into the cliff face here. As at many sites in Mesa Verde, there are also hand- and toe-holds chiselled into the face of the cliff. However, it is the stone steps at the south end of the alcove that gave this site its modern name.

LONG HOUSE

With 21 kivas and 150 rooms in three stories, Long House is the second largest cliff dwelling in the park. It has a good seep spring and could have accommodated almost two hundred people. Recent thinking, however, is that Long House may have been a ceremonial center that was occupied year-round by only a small group of caretakers. There is a dance plaza in front that resembles those where ceremonies are carried out in Hopi pueblos today.

BADGER HOUSE COMMUNITY

The trail through the Badger House Community leads to four sites spanning six centuries of settlement. The first site, a pithouse, dates from around AD 650. The second site is from the Developmental Pueblo or Pueblo I period and shows how the people were building their single-room homes above ground in curved rows, sharing masonry walls with their neighbors on either side. Because Badger House was built in two phases, it illustrates differences between Pueblo II and III: the later masonry is double-coursed and more finely chiseled. The tunnel connecting tower and kiva here is the longest one known. Two Raven House is a Pueblo II village with traces of a brush fence that may have confined turkeys or toddlers to the vicinity of the house.

KODAK HOUSE (OVERLOOK)

A short trail leads to a view of Rock Canyon and Kodak House, a cliff dwelling so-named because it is where Gustav Nordenskiold stashed his camera rather than carry it up and down the canyon walls.

OPPOSITE: Ladders and walls at Long House. PHOTO © STEVE MOHLENCAMP

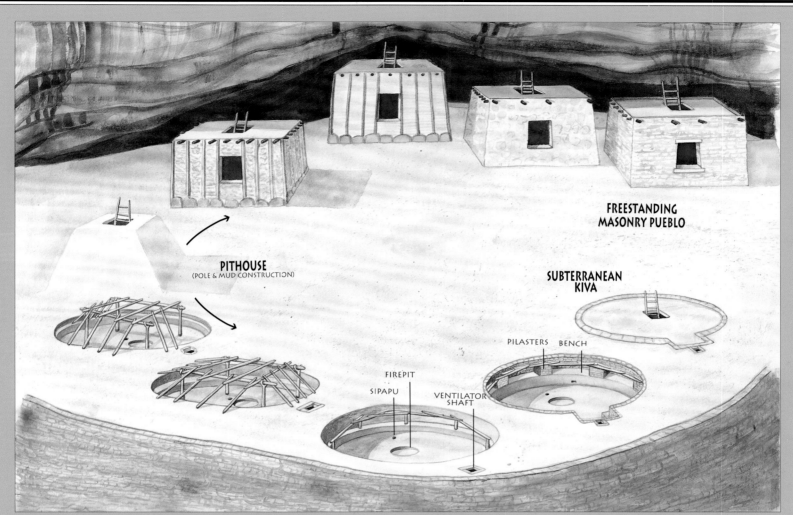

Illustration showing how the pithouse gradually evolved into kivas and free-standing masonry pueblos.

ILLUSTRATION BY DARLECE CLEVELAND

Labels within illustration: FREESTANDING MASONRY PUEBLO; PITHOUSE (POLE & MUD CONSTRUCTION); SUBTERRANEAN KIVA; PILASTERS; BENCH; FIREPIT; SIPAPU; VENTILATOR SHAFT

PITHOUSES AND KIVAS

"Pueblo" is a Spanish word that can mean people, building, or community. These concepts have been interchangeable among Puebloan people since at least AD 750, when their dwellings began to reflect a society that lived, worked, and even prayed collectively.

Architecture at Mesa Verde begins and ends with structures incorporated into the stony mesa itself: the pithouse and the cliff dwelling. A pithouse was a large room plus an antechamber, both dug half-way into the ground where they were well insulated from the heat or cold. The upper walls were of *jacal*—woven brush and mud—that sloped inward, supporting a log roof with corner posts. People entered through a hole in the center of this flat roof, by a ladder propped over a hearth in the middle of the floor. Most pithouse communities also had several outside storage rooms made of jacal.

At the outset of Pueblo I (c. 750), the jacal rooms were probably enlarged and used as shelter during warm weather, while people still retreated to the pithouses in winter. Before long, however, most people lived year-round in above-ground rooms with shared walls of adobe or stone, often constructed in a row curved around a central plaza and oriented to the south or southwest to take advantage of the sun's warmth

in winter. In the plaza, there was commonly a subterranean room much like a pithouse. Small clay figurines and pipes for smoking wild tobacco indicate that these were early *kivas*, the kind of ceremonial chambers still in use by Puebloan people for community discussions, tradition-bound activities such as weaving, and ceremonies. Kivas have many features in common with pithouses, including a bench around the walls and a hole in the floor north of the hearth. This hole is called a *sipapu* by the Hopi. It represents the passageway through which the first people entered this world.

By mid-Pueblo II (c. 1075), walls were thicker, with double-courses of stone to support a second story of rooms. Mortar came from the banks of streams far below in the canyons. Large, complex communities with numerous pueblos developed, some with kivas connected by underground passages to high stone towers. There was considerable investment of time and labor in these later pueblos, and many were modified over time.

During the Classic phase, masons shaped sandstone for building by chiseling or "pecking" it into blocks with stone axes. Individuals did such distinctive work that archaeologists of today can tell which mason built which part of a wall. Around 1200, many people moved into south-facing cliff alcoves, where the solid rock was both support and insulation for their dwellings.

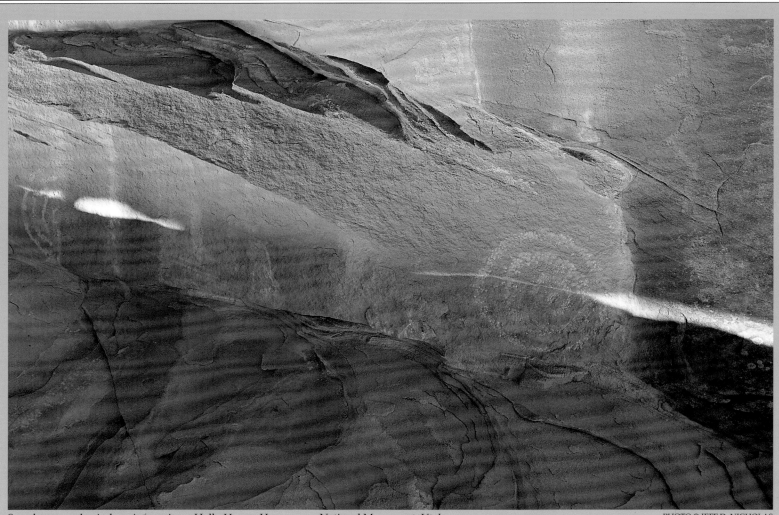

Sun-dagger and spiral, spring equinox, Holly House, Hovenweep National Monument, Utah. PHOTO © JEFF D. NICHOLAS

ARCHAEO-ASTRONOMY

Because the air is so clear, the stars over Mesa Verde are so bright they seem to crackle and the constellations appear in three dimensions. We can almost feel the earth wheeling through the night and then, as the sun begins to rise, the eastern horizon lightens to mauve and birds burst into song. Within moments, warmth suffuses the air.

Archaeoastronomers have found a number of observatories where ancestral Puebloan people kept track of where the sun or moon rose on the horizon. They may have done this in order to coordinate ceremonies. Like their modern counterparts, they probably understood that the sun's light and warmth are essential to plants, which in turn sustain humans and other animals. It would have been only natural to encourage the sun to return from its farthest point on the horizon at the winter solstice, for example. The summer solstice would also have been of great significance, for it heralds the longed-for rains of July and August on the Colorado Plateau. Sunrise at certain points along the horizon may also have prompted the planting of specific crops in the past, as it prompts Puebloan farmers today.

How did these observatories work? In some cases, an observer watched the point of sunrise move along the horizon each day in relation to a distant feature such as a butte, until it reached a maximum point to the north or south and reversed direction in the following days. At other places, the observer looked *away* from the sun to see whether its shadow had reached a mark on a wall or boulder to indicate the solstice. For example, a spiral petroglyph at Hovenweep's Holly House is touched on the spring equinox by a dagger of light from the rising sun.

Ancestral Puebloans marked the movements of the moon as well. Archeoastronomers believe that a window in the square tower at Cliff House tracked the lunar standstill, a celestial event similar to the solstice that occurs only once in a human generation.

The stars change position in the night sky, too, depending upon the season. Conspicuous constellations and planets such as Venus, the Morning Star, are clearly depicted on ancient Puebloan pottery, walls, and boulders.

Petroglyphs and pictographs in many areas suggest that the ancestral Puebloans also noted extraordinary astronomical events including supernovae, sunspots, and eclipses. As people have in other parts of the world, ancestral Puebloans may have attributed difficulties such as drought to these events and performed prayers or ceremonies when they occurred again.

OPPOSITE: Square tower at Cliff Palace. PHOTO © ERIC WUNROW

THE FIRES OF 2000

I wrote this book during the summer of 2000. Every morning I checked the *Denver Post Online* for an update on the Bircher and Pony Fires. For weeks, the news was crushing. The weather continued hot, dry, and windy; first one and then the other fire kept shifting direction and roaring across more of the mesa. It was the same all across the West: people evacuated from their homes and miles of scenic country scarred for at least the rest of my lifetime. I couldn't bear to think about wildlife unable to outrun flames that extended three hundred feet.

I talked it over with Jane, a Hopi friend.

"You know, in our belief," she said, "when we start to use the world instead of taking care of it, things are going to happen. And it won't be like last time, when there was a big flood. They always said next time it would be fire."

Jane's comments often have this teacherly quality, this insistence upon cause and effect. But her reasons for why things happen are seldom what a person of my culture would assume. She believes it is our intentions that shape the outcome of our efforts, not our technical skills or our ability to manage. Another time, for instance, she and I were together in her husband's ancient clan house, which has no electricity. It was late afternoon and Jane was filling a kerosene lamp. She made an off-hand remark about a political figure that was funny but not very charitable. Suddenly, kerosene slopped onto the wooden table. She looked up at me, abashed.

"I shouldn't have been talking like that," she apologized. "I've filled this lamp so many times, but look so what happened!"

There is a huge gulf between Jane's world and mine. When we of European descent visit Mesa Verde—which was inhabited continuously for more than 700 years—we invariably ask, "Why did they leave?" We seem sure that our science could conquer any problems the ancestral Puebloans might have had. Yet it is doubtful that the ancestral Puebloans experienced any catastrophic wildfires. They did not suppress the natural fire cycle and, as archaeologists point out, they used dead wood for cooking and heating.

Forest ecologists have been saying that catastrophic fires are inevitable unless we thin the forest, remove dead wood and duff, and set controlled burns during cool, calm weather to reduce the dangerously high fuel load. Most of us know by now that fire is part of a natural cycle that restores nutrients to the soil, removes debris inhibiting other plants, and weeds out seedlings that if allowed to grow, would compete with existing shrubs and trees. As ancestral Puebloans gleaned the landscape for fuel, they cleared it so that grasses, herbs, and shrubs browsed by deer and rabbits could receive light and moisture. Puebloan people still maintain what they believe is a mutually beneficial relationship with nature. Enrique Salmón, an ethnobotanist at Fort Lewis College in Durango, challenges the prevailing notion that the Southwest was an untouched wilderness until Spanish conquistadors arrived.

"We've always attended to the plants and animals around us," he says. "People have a place in nature; the problems start when we forget this."

So should we be out in the forest raking pine needles and picking up sticks in return for what the forest provides? Perhaps we would be wise to at least learn about our natural environment and support efforts to keep it healthy.

Along the park road, visitors can see where fires burned in 1934, 1959, 1972, 1989, and 1996. These areas are recovering. In the summer of 2000, lightning ignited two fires that burned so furiously that parts of the mesa once cloaked in pinyon-juniper forest may not recover for three hundred years. Without a shred of vegetation to hold the soil in place, erosion began to eat away at the foundations of archaeological sites and scatter their artifacts.

I visited Mesa Verde a few weeks after the fires. I was with friends and, at first, we chattered with animation about the extent of the damage. We thought it was interesting to see the soil, to scuff at it with our boots and see how deeply it had been baked and sterilized. It had rained the night before and the air was dense with the reek of soggy charcoal. All at once it hit us and we felt inexpressibly weary. There had been so much

ABOVE: Badger House Community following the Pony Fire of 2000, Wetherill Mesa. PHOTO © JEFF D. NICHOLAS

death on Wetherill Mesa. Where once there had been a forest alive with the fragrance of flowering shrubs and with the twittering, scurrying, and rustling of creatures, there was now a moonscape with only blackened skeletons of trees twisting grotesquely into the pale sky.

On Thursday, July 20, lightning started the Bircher Fire on private land just outside the entrance to the park. A fire crew responded immediately and visitors to the park were evacuated. Winds quickly whipped the fire up onto the mesa. The Incident Command System—a uniform protocol for determining fire behavior and the risk it poses—required that the firefighters withdraw to safer ground temporarily but soon there were crews heroically defending Mesa Verde. Sunday, they managed to save the landscape and facilities around Morefield Campground.

More than 1,000 firefighters from 28 states and Puerto Rico fought the Bircher Fire at a cost of $5.5 million. It was finally contained on July 29, having burned almost 20,000 acres within the park.

Mesa Verde re-opened on August 4, but closed after just 12 hours. The Pony Fire, ignited August 2 on neighboring Ute land, was raging out of control. On Saturday, it burned over Wetherill Mesa, destroyed the visitor facilities there, and damaged coverings that protected mesa-top sites. Flames licked several of the alcoves and flakes of sandstone began to spall off of the natural rim over Step House. That Sunday the fire threatened Chapin Mesa: park headquarters, housing, concessions, museum, research center, and

a collection of 2.5 million artifacts. Firefighters cleared vegetation to lessen the danger but it was a change in wind and an increase in humidity that averted disaster.

The Pony Fire was contained August 11; the park re-opened August 14. This fire burned more than 1,300 acres of the national park as well as nearly 4,000 acres of Ute land equally rich in archaeological sites. More than 500 firefighters from 19 states and Mexico battled the Pony Fire at a cost of $2.6 million.

The fires burned land managed by different jurisdictions—local, county, state, tribal, and federal—which combined personnel, equipment, and expertise to fight them. Later, officials compiled an "incident review" of the Bircher Fire based upon radio dispatches, on-site logs, and photographs in order to improve coordination of future firefighting efforts. In the aftermath of the Pony Fire, the National Park Service and the Ute Mountain Ute Nation—two-thirds of the mesa is Ute land—plan to work together to document sites and rehabilitate the natural environment.

After the fires, a federal Burned Area Emergency Rehabilitation (BAER) Team prepared a plan to mitigate the damage. Seven hundred acres of Mexican spotted owl territory burned, together with habitat for other species, including golden eagles, red-spotted toads and various fishes whose canyon-bottom creeks may receive an increase of dirt and ash, and mammals such as bats, shrews, and voles. Another concern is that non-native plants may invade burned areas to the detriment of native plants and the insects, birds, and other animals that live in community with them. Mitigation will entail re-seeding 6,000 acres with native grasses, digging ditches and installing culverts to control erosion, and keeping an eye on other potential problems. As many as 2,000 previously unrecorded archaeological sites may have been exposed. Although it has been suggested that this might be one positive result of the fires, park archeologists know that the damage from these fires far outweighed the importance of any information to be gained from new sites.

As you approach the museum, visitor services, headquarters, and housing area on Chapin Mesa, observe the belt of pinyon-juniper forest that surrounds it. Crews thinned and groomed the forest here. It was an expensive undertaking, but far less costly to taxpayers—and to the forest and archaeological sites—than the cost and destruction of a major fire. If there is any positive result of the fires of 2000, it is that we may now appreciate the value of stewardship in our relationship with the forest.

ABOVE: Vegetation recovery following the Chapin 5 Fire of 1996, Chapin Mesa. PHOTO © TOM BEAN

Archaeologist Jesse Walter Fewkes outside the park's first museum with artifacts recovered at Mesa Verde, 1917.   *PHOTO COURTESY NPS, MESA VERDE COLLECTION

THE ANTIQUITIES ACT OF 1906

Archaeological sites are not renewable resources. Once dwellings and artifacts have been disturbed, the potential information from their context and stratigraphy is lost forever. Fortunately, federal laws now protect the antiquities on our public lands from careless destruction or exploitation.

Archaeology in the United States dates back to 1784, when Thomas Jefferson systematically excavated an ancient mound in Virginia. The country had only just won its political independence and the ensuing fascination with archaeology has been seen as an effort to establish a sense of cultural independence from Europe. Be that as it may, the establishment of the Smithsonian Institution in 1846 provided a home base for archaeological research as well as a repository for data and artifacts. In 1879, both the Bureau of Ethnology and the Archeological Institute of America were founded. These organizations eventually set the standards for professional activities in the field.

With increasing public interest in antiquities came a problem: the ransacking of sites to obtain artifacts for sale. In 1882, legislation to protect antiquities on federal lands was introduced but failed to pass, due to concern that it would be unenforceable in the sparsely settled West.

However, the problem worsened and on June 8, 1906, Congress finally passed legislation known as the Antiquities Act, making it a federal offense to "appropriate, excavate, injure, or destroy any historic or prehistoric ruin or monument, or any object of antiquity" on federal land. The Antiquities Act also authorized the President to declare federal lands as national monuments on the basis of their cultural resources. In 1916, Congress passed the "Organic Act," by which national parks are created through legislative action rather than by presidential decree.

Several other laws clarify and enhance the effect of these two acts. One of the most significant is the Native American Graves Protection and Repatriation Act of 1990 (NAGPRA). This act further defines illegal trafficking in Native American remains and artifacts. It also mandates that each federal agency and museum that has Native American "objects of cultural patrimony" must compile an inventory of these items and determine the geographical and cultural affiliation of each one. The tribal originators of objects that are now in federal possession must be notified and their artifacts returned if requested. NAGPRA has brought American archaeology full circle, reuniting tribal people with their heritage. It has also created new opportunities for communication between Native Americans and those who study their past.

*Photograph digitally altered, at the request of the National Park Service, to eliminate culturally sensitive material.

RESOURCES & INFORMATION

EMERGENCY & MEDICAL:
24-HOUR EMERGENCY MEDICAL SERVICE
Dial 911 (From hotel rooms dial 9-911)

ROAD CONDITIONS:
MESA VERDE	(970) 529-4461
ARIZONA	(520) 779-2711
COLORADO	(303) 639-1111
NEW MEXICO	(800) 432-4269
UTAH	(801) 964-6000

FOR MORE INFORMATION:
NATIONAL PARKS ON THE INTERNET:
www.nps.gov

MESA VERDE NATIONAL PARK
PO Box 8
Mesa Verde National Park, CO 81330
(970) 529-4465, TDD (970) 529-4633
www.nps.gov/meve
(Complete Interpretive Schedule—
Memorial Day through Labor Day)

MESA VERDE MUSEUM ASSOCIATION
PO Box 38
Mesa Verde, CO 81330
(800) 305-6053, (970) 529-4445

LODGING INSIDE THE PARK:
ARAMARK MESA VERDE
(Open mid-April through mid-October)
PO Box 277
Mancos, CO 81328
(970) 529-4421, (800) 449-2288
www.visitmesaverde.com

CAMPING INSIDE THE PARK:
ARAMARK MESA VERDE
PO Box 277
Mancos, CO 81328
(970) 529-4421, (800) 449-2288
www.visitmesaverde.com

LODGING OUTSIDE THE PARK:
MESA VERDE COUNTRY
VISITOR INFORMATION BUREAU
PO Drawer HH
Cortez, CO 81321
(800) 253-1616
www.swcolo.org

OTHER REGIONAL SITES:
ANASAZI HERITAGE CENTER
27501 Highway 184
Dolores, CO 82323
(970) 882-4811
www.co.blm.gov/ahc/hmepge.htm

ARCHES NATIONAL PARK
(435) 586-9451
www.nps.gov/arch

AZTEC RUINS NATIONAL MONUMENT
(505) 334-6174
www.nps.gov/azru/

BANDELIER NATIONAL MONUMENT
(505) 672-0343
www.nps.gov/band/

CANYON DE CHELLY NATIONAL MONUMENT
(520) 674-5500
www.nps.gov/cach/

CANYONLANDS NATIONAL PARK
(435) 719-2313
www.nps.gov/cany/

CAPITOL REEF NATIONAL PARK
(435) 425-3791
www.nps.gov/care

CHACO CULTURE NATIONAL HISTORICAL PARK
(505) 786-7014

CHIMNEY ROCK ARCHAEOLOGICAL AREA
(970) 883-5359, 385-1210
www.chimneyrockco.org

CORTEZ CENTER ARCHAEOLOGICAL MUSEUM
25 N. Market St., Cortez, CO 81321
(970) 565-1151

CROW CANYON ARCHAEOLOGICAL CENTER
23390 County Rd K, Cortez, CO 81321
(800) 422-8975

EL MALPAIS NATIONAL MONUMENT
(505) 287-7911 Grants Field
(505) 240-0300 El Malpais Ranger Station
www.nps.gov/elma

EL MORRO NATIONAL MONUMENT
(505) 783-4226
www.nps.gov/elmo/

GLEN CANYON NATIONAL RECREATION AREA
(505) 608-6404
www.nps.gov/glca/

HOPI CULTURAL CENTER
PO Box 67, Second Mesa, AZ 86043
(520) 734-2401

HOVENWEEP NATIONAL MONUMENT
(970) 562-4282
WWW.NPS.GOV/HOVE/

MONTEZUMA CASTLE NATIONAL MONUMENT
(520) 567-3322
www.nps.gov/moca

MONUMENT VALLEY NAVAJO TRIBAL PARK
PO Box 360289
Monument Valley, UT 84536
(435) 727-3353 or 727-3287

NAVAJO NATIONAL MONUMENT
(520) 672-2366/2367
www.nps.gov/nava

PETRIFIED FOREST NATIONAL PARK
(520) 524-6228
www.nps.gov/pefo

PUEBLO CULTURAL CENTER
2401 12th Street NW, Albuquerque, NM 87104
(800) 766-4405

SOUTHERN UTE INDIAN CULTURAL CENTER
Hwy 172
Ignacio, CO 81337
(970) 563-4641, Museum Store (970) 563-4649

UTE MOUNTAIN TRIBAL PARK
Towaoc, CO 81334
(970) 565-3751 ext 282, or 565-4684

WUPATKI NATIONAL MONUMENT
(520) 679-2365
www.nps.gov/wupa/

SUGGESTED READING:

Adams, Charles. *THE ORIGIN AND DEVELOPMENT OF THE PUEBLO KATSINA CULT.* 1991. University of Arizona Press.

Adler, Michael (editor). *THE PREHISTORIC PUEBLO WORLD, AD 1150-1350.* 1996. University of Arizona Press.

Cheek, Lawrence. *AD 1250, ANCIENT PEOPLE OF THE SOUTHWEST.* 1994. Arizona Highways.

Cole, Sally. *LEGACY ON STONE: ROCK ART OF THE COLORADO PLATEAU AND FOUR CORNERS REGION.* 1990. Johnson Books.

Lister, Florence C. and Robert H. Lister. *THOSE WHO CAME BEFORE.* (1983). Reprint. Tucson, AZ: Southwest Parks and Monuments Assoc. 1989.

Malville, J. McKim and Claudia Putnam. *PREHISTORIC ASTRONOMY IN THE SOUTHWEST.* 1989. Johnson Books.

Nordenskiold, Gustav. *THE CLIFF DWELLERS OF THE MESA VERDE.* 1893. Mesa Verde Museum Association.

Oppelt, Norman T. *EARTH, WATER, AND FIRE: THE PREHISTORIC POTTERY OF MESA VERDE.* 1991. Johnson books.

Ortiz, Alfonso. *THE HANDBOOK OF NORTH AMERICAN INDIANS, VOLUME 9:* Washington, DC: Smithsonian Institution. 1979.

Schaafsma, Polly. *INDIAN ART ROCK OF THE SOUTHWEST:* Albuquerque, NM: University of New Mexico Press. 1990.

Smith, Jack. *MESAS, CLIFFS, AND CANYONS: UNIVERSITY OF COLORADO SURVEY OF MESA VERDE NATIONAL PARK 1971-1977.* 1987. Mesa Verde Museum Association.

ACKNOWLEDGMENTS:

I thank the staff of Mesa Verde National Park, especially Larry Nordby, Will Morris, Linda Martin, Mona Hutchinson, and Cherie Barth for their help in researching and reviewing the manuscript. I am also grateful to Tracey and Rovilla of the Mesa Verde Museum Association for their insights, and to Martha Blue, Patricia Wolf Hoenshell, Jack Doggett, and Kay Whitham of Flagstaff for their perceptive comments on the draft. My thanks to Jeff Nicholas, also, for his attention and encouragement throughout the project.   —S.L.

The publisher would like to thank Will Morris, Chief of Interpretation, and his staff for their invaluable assistance. Special thanks are also due to Tracey Hobson, Shirley Jones, and Rovilla Ellis at the Mesa Verde Museum Association. As always, thanks to the talented photographers who shared their visions with me in the production of this book and a special thanks to Susan Lamb and Tom Bean for their contributions to this publication.   —J.D.N.

PRODUCTION CREDITS:

Publisher: Jeff D. Nicholas
Author: Susan Lamb
Editor: Nicky Leach
Photo Editors: Jeff D. Nicholas and
                    Marcia Huskey
Illustrations: Darlece Cleveland
Illustrations Graphics: Marcia Huskey
Printing Coordination: Sung In Printing America

ISBN 1-58071-031-X (Paper), 1-58071-032-8 (Cloth)
©2001 Panorama International Productions, Inc.
4988 Gold Leaf Drive
Mariposa, CA 95338

Printed in the Republic of South Korea.
First printing, Spring 2001.

SIERRA PRESS

4988 Gold Leaf Drive
Mariposa, CA 95338
(209) 966-5071, 966-5073 (Fax)
e-mail: siepress@yosemite.net

VISIT OUR WEBSITE AT:
www.nationalparksusa.com

SIERRA PRESS

OPPOSITE:
East-facing Balcony House, early morning.
PHOTO © LAURENCE PARENT